Book #3 of THE *ViBE* CONFIDENCE-BUILDING SERIES FOR KIDS,
Ages 7 to 12 (or younger with adult support)

FEEL THE ViBE AT CAMP

An Interactive Workbook of CAMP-RELATED FUN Activities to Encourage YOU to Do, Read, Think, Draw, and Write....
Including a Focus on LETTER-WRITING Made Easy
*Great for DAY CAMP & SLEEP-AWAY CAMP

MARNIE and RENA SCHWARTZ

Copyright @ViBE Studio Productions Inc., 2022
All Rights Reserved.

ISBN 978-1-7779867-9-7

No part of this book may be reproduced or transmitted in any form or by any means, electronic or mechanical, including photocopying, recording, or by an information storage or retrieval system, without permission in writing from the authors, Marnie or Rena Schwartz at info@vibestudio.ca

If you are a teacher or camp counselor and would like to use the pages of this book with your students, please visit TEACHERS PAY TEACHERS at www.teacherspayteachers.com/ to purchase a downloadable copy.

DEDICATION

This book is dedicated to anyone
who wants to have FUN and gain CONFIDENCE!

THIS BOOK BELONGS TO

_____

TABLE OF CONTENTS

WHY WE WROTE THIS BOOK   1
I'm off to camp and am looking forward to: 3
DRAWING ACTIVITY - HERE'S ME!   4
Today's CAMP activities included: 5
ALL ABOUT ME!   6
INTERVIEW A NEW FRIEND   7
INTERVIEW THE SAME NEW FRIEND (OR A DIFFERENT NEW FRIEND)   8
INTERVIEW YOUR CAMP COUNSELOR   9
PLAY NAME BINGO   11
DRAWING ACTIVITY - CAMP FUN   15
DOODLE PAGE   16
RECORD & RATE YOUR CAMP ACTIVITIES   17
MINI SCAVENGER HUNT   19
WRITE OR DRAW   21
BEST JOKES I HEARD AT CAMP   23
A TYPICAL CAMP SCHEDULE   24
WRITE ONE OR MORE CAMP-RELATED WORDS FOR EACH LETTER   25
CREATE AN ACROSTIC POEM   27
CREATE YOUR OWN ACROSTIC POEMS   28
A TIME TO DRAW & SKETCH   30
HOW MANY POINTS?   31

WORD GAME   33
DRAWING & STORYTELLING   35
WHY DOES A LEADER NEED TO BE A LEARNER? LET'S WRITE...   39
TODAY I AM GRATEFUL FOR...LET'S WRITE...   40
WHAT ARE YOU CONFIDENT DOING? Draw or write.   41
CAN YOU CARTWHEEL?   42
CAN YOU DRAW CARTWHEELS?   43
CHECK OUT THE CARTWHIRLER   44
MY JOURNAL PAGES   45
LETTER-WRITING MADE EASY!   49
STEPS TO LETTER-WRITING   50
TO WHOM SHALL I WRITE MY LETTER?   51
LETTER-WRITING TEMPLATES   52
DRAW OR SKETCH   68
WHAT CAN I DRAW OR SKETCH TO ADD TO MY LETTERS?   69
BLANK PAGES FOR DRAWING OR SKETCHING   70
CAMP MEMORIES   82
AUTOGRAPHS   84
WOW! YOU DID A LOT OF FUN THINGS AT CAMP!   88
FEEL THE ViBE AT CAMP THIS SUMMER!   89
ACKNOWLEDMENTS   90
ABOUT THE AUTHORS   91
LET'S ViBE TOGETHER   92

WHY WE WROTE THIS BOOK

I'm Marnie Schwartz. I'm Rena Schwartz. We are identical adult twins. We LOVE to dance, cartwheel, and draw. We own a dance studio for ALL dancers. We run **CAMP ViBE** during the summer months.
Our goal is to inspire children and teens to believe in themselves, build confidence, and become the best they can be.
At our dance studio and summer camp, everyone is welcome, accepted, respected, and treated like they are #1.
We believe that being able to *dance*, *cartwheel*, *think*, *read*, *write*, *draw*, *play game*s, and *make friends* builds confidence and self-esteem.
It teaches you to be powerful, strong, independent, happy, and capable of doing anything. It teaches you to cooperate, collaborate, and work as a team.

Together, we are on a mission to ignite CONFIDENCE in kids...

one *dance* at a time....
one *cartwheel* at a time....
one *picture* at a time....
one *activity* at a time....
one *game* at a time....
one *story* at a time....
one *experience* at a time....

As part of **THE *ViBE* CONFIDENCE-BUILDING SERIES FOR KIDS,
Ages 7 to 12 (or younger with adult support)**,
this WORKBOOK contains suggestions to encourage YOU
to do, read, think, draw, and write to help you
REFLECT on all the FUN things you are doing at
CAMP (either at a ***day camp*** or a ***sleep-away camp***).

Remember to have your pencils and markers on hand.

This book also contains **TEMPLATES** to help
make **CAMP LETTER-WRITING Easy and Fun!**
All you need are **stamps** and some **stickers** to close the
Do-It-Yourself (DIY) envelopes in this book
after you **FOLD** along the dotted lines and tear/cut out the pages.

The **sentence starters** make it a simple way to write letters
to all of your family members and friends.

This is especially useful if you are at a ***sleep-away camp.***

Date: _____

I'm off to camp and am looking forward to: _____

_____

_____.

My camp is called:_____.

It is located at _____.

I am feeling _____ *(excited, happy, energized, other....)* **about being at camp!**

Yah!!!

DRAWING ACTIVITY - HERE'S ME!

Draw a **PORTRAIT** of yourself!
(Remember that a portrait is a close-up picture of YOU including only your face, head, and shoulders.)

Date: _____

Today's CAMP activities included:

_____

_____

_____

_____

_____

_____

_____

_____

_____

ALL ABOUT ME!

My name is _____.

My age is _____.

My birthday is _____.

My hair colour is _____.

My eye colour is _____.

My favorite colour is _____.

The song I like best is _____.

The dance I enjoy most is_____.

My most-loved game is _____.

The camp activity I love to do is _____

because_____.

INTERVIEW A NEW FRIEND

What is your name? _____.

When is your birthday? _____.

What is your favorite colour? _____.

What book did you just recently read that you liked? _____

_____.

What movie or TV program have you recently watched that you liked? _____.

What song do you enjoy? _____.

What dance do you like? _____.

What is your best camp activity so far? _____

_____.

INTERVIEW THE SAME NEW FRIEND
OR A DIFFERENT NEW FRIEND

Where were you born? _____.

How many sisters and/or brothers do you have? _____.

What school do you go to? _____.

What are your best subjects in school? _____

_____.

What activities or sports do you participate in during the school year? _____

_____.

What do you love to eat for breakfast? _____.

What do you love to eat for lunch? _____.

What is the snack you enjoy the most? _____.

INTERVIEW YOUR CAMP COUNSELOR

What is your name? _____.

When is your birthday? _____.

What is your most-loved colour? _____.

What food do you like to eat?_____.

What song do you enjoy? _____.

What dance do you like?_____.

What is your best camp activity? _____

_____.

What do you enjoy about being a camp counselor? _____

_____.

INTERVIEW YOUR CAMP COUNSELOR
(CONTINUED)

Where were you born? _____

_____.

How many sisters and/or brothers do you have? _____.

What school do you go to? _____.

What do you do for fun and why do you like it? _____

_____.

What are you good at doing? _____

_____

What is your passion? _____.

What is your career goal? _____.

PLAY NAME BINGO

This is a great way to find out more about your camp friends.

Play with a group. Use one of the next few pages, or take a blank sheet of paper and fold it into the appropriate number of squares to create your BINGO card.

1. Decide how many people are playing with you.
2. Walk around and meet up with one person at a time, and write his/her name in one of your boxes plus **include one fact** about that person that they tell you when you meet up. For example: *Alex has a dog named Crosby*. Write this fact in the box with the person's name.
3. When you are done, write each player's name on slips of paper and put into a box, and play **BINGO**. That is, when a name is picked out of the box and called, if you have that person's name on your card, check it off....PLUS each person, one at a time, reads out loud the facts they have on their card about that person. In this way, everyone finds out more about each person.
4. When the names on your card are completely checked off (e.g., across one line, down one line, a T-shape, etc. to be decided in advance), you become the winner and you can call **BINGO**.

IMPORTANT: Each time you meet up with a new friend, you each need to give a *different* fact. You may want to brainstorm facts about yourselves before you begin this game. Also, if only a few people are playing, you should use the card with the 6 boxes and you can meet up with the same person a few times.

DRAWING ACTIVITY - CAMP FUN

Draw a picture of yourself doing something fun at camp.

DOODLE PAGE

RECORD & RATE YOUR CAMP ACTIVITIES

How did you enjoy each activity?
On the line beside each of the activities that you did,
RATE with a number from 1-5, with 5 as the best!

CAMP ACTIVITIES & RATING:

Arts and Crafts _____
Baseball _____
Dance _____
Drama _____
Gymnastics _____
Hiking _____
Music and Singing _____
Performing _____
Playing games _____
Relay races _____
Obstacle courses _____
Soccer _____
Tie Dye _____
Other _____ _____

RECORD & RATE YOUR CAMP ACTIVITIES

How did you enjoy each one?
On the line beside each of the activities that you did,
RATE with a number from 1-5, with 5 as the best!

CAMP ACTIVITIES & RATING:

_____   _____

_____   _____

_____   _____

_____   _____

_____   _____

_____   _____

_____   _____

MINI SCAVENGER HUNT

Put a check below if you see someone....

____ wearing a blue top
____ with a pony tail
____ with a bracelet
____ with earrings
____ wearing a hat
____ wearing a shirt with a sports team name on it
____ wearing a t-shirt with a funny saying on it
____ eating a sandwich
____ playing with a ball
____ running
____ jumping
____ skipping
____ laughing
____ singing
____ dancing
____ cartwheeling
____ other: _____

Count the number of checks you have within a specific period of time.

MINI SCAVENGER HUNT

Create your own mini scavenger hunt.

Decide in advance (with a partner or group) a list of things to search for.
Put a check below if you see each one.
Count the number of checks you have within a specific period of time.

____ _____

____ _____

____ _____

____ _____

____ _____

____ _____

____ _____

____ _____

____ _____

____ _____

WRITE OR DRAW

At camp, I see something that is **RED**.

WRITE OR DRAW

At camp, I see something that is **YELLOW**.

BEST JOKES I HEARD AT CAMP

A TYPICAL CAMP SCHEDULE

Here's what a typical day at camp looks like:

TIME　　**ACTIVITY**

_____　　_____

_____　　_____

_____　　_____

_____　　_____

_____　　_____

_____　　_____

My best activity so far is: _____.

WRITE ONE OR MORE CAMP-RELATED WORDS FOR EACH LETTER

Follow our lead. We did a few examples.

A *is for* **A**ction packed days
B *is for* **B**eing the **B**est we can **B**e
C *is for* _____
D *is for* _____
E *is for* _____
F *is for* _____
G *is for* _____
H *is for* _____
I *is for* _____
J *is for* _____
K *is for* _____
L *is for* _____
M *is for* _____

WRITE ONE OR MORE CAMP-RELATED WORDS FOR EACH LETTER

N *is for* **N**ever being mean
O *is for* **O**nly do good things
P *is for* _____
Q *is for* _____
R *is for* _____
S *is for* _____
T *is for* _____
U *is for* _____
V *is for* _____
W *is for* _____
X *is for* _____
Y *is for* _____
Z *is for* _____

CREATE AN ACROSTIC POEM

Follow the pattern below.

Use your name or the name of someone you like: **SUSAN**

S *is for* _____
U *is for* _____
S *is for* _____
A *is for* _____
N *is for* _____

Use the name of a camp activity that you like: **DANCE**

D *is for* _____
A *is for* _____
N *is for* _____
C *is for* _____
E *is for* _____

CREATE YOUR OWN ACROSTIC POEMS

CREATE YOUR OWN ACROSTIC POEMS

A TIME TO DRAW & SKETCH

What ideas do you have?

HOW MANY POINTS?

Letters can be numbers!
Figure out how many points each word is worth. (We know you can.)

**Write the numeric value underneath each letter
and add them up to find the total. Have fun.**

A = 1   B = 2   C = 3   D = 4   E = 5   F = 6   G = 7   H = 8   I = 9
J = 10   K = 11   L = 12   M = 13   N = 14   O = 15   P = 16   Q = 17   R = 18
S = 19   T = 20   U = 21   V = 22   W = 23   X = 24   Y = 25   Z = 26

Here's an example for you:

D   A   N   C   E
4   1   14   3   5   Soooo....
4 + 1 + 14 + 3 + 5 = 27

The total for the word **DANCE** is **27**

C   A   M   P   =

__   __   __   __   _____

E   X   C   I   T   E   M   E   N   T =

__   __   __   __   __   __   __   __   __   _____

HOW MANY POINTS?

Letters can be numbers!
Figure out how many points each word is worth.

**Write the numeric value underneath each letter
and add them up to find the total. Have fun.**

A = 1   B = 2   C = 3   D = 4   E = 5   F = 6   G = 7   H = 8   I = 9
J = 10 K = 11 L = 12 M = 13 N = 14 O = 15 P = 16 Q = 17 R = 18
S = 19 T = 20 U = 21 V = 22 W = 23 X = 24 Y = 25 Z = 26

**CREATE YOUR OWN WORDS AND ADD UP THE POINTS.
SHARE WITH A FRIEND.**

WORD GAME

Create as many words as you can from the following **3** words by rearranging the letters into any order.
How many words can you make?
We did a few for you.

ENTHUSIASTIC CAMP FUN

- us
- as
- is
- ten
- tan
- the
- enthusiasm
-
-
-
-
-
-
-
-
-

-
-
-
-
-
-
-
-
-
-

WORD GAME

Create as many words as you can from the following **5** words by rearranging the letters into any order.
How many words can you make?
We did a few for you.

FEEL THE *ViBE* AT CAMP

- am
- amp
- lamp
-
-
-
-
-
-
-
-
-
-

-
-
-
-
-

DRAWING & STORYTELLING

Draw a picture of 3 things:

1. **YOU**
2. an **animal** (e.g., a snake, a dog, an elephant, a bird, a mouse)
3. a **building** (e.g., a school, a dance studio, an apartment building, the Toronto CN Tower)

YOU are the *main character*. The **animal** helps to create the *plot* because something happens between the animal and YOU. The **building** sets the scene and becomes the *setting*.

As you draw, **create a story in your mind:**

- Imagine that YOU are standing *in front of*, *behind*, *on the roof,* or *in* the building. (This is the *setting*.)
- Imagine that you are interacting with the animal and that something (*interesting, scary, funny, sad, etc.*) happens. (This is the *plot*.)

Using your picture, **tell** your story to a partner.

Have fun drawing & storytelling!

DRAWING & STORYTELLING

DRAWING & STORYTELLING

What was your story about?

- Where did your story take place? What was the **setting**?
- What **animal** did you choose to be in your story?
- ***Tell*** your story by looking at your picture.
    - How did your story start? (*beginning*)
    - What happened? (*middle*)
    - How did it end? (*ending*)

How easy was it to *tell* your story after drawing your picture?

What did you learn about storytelling?

DRAWING & STORYTELLING

What other stories can you draw and tell?

WHY DOES A LEADER NEED TO BE A LEARNER?

LET'S WRITE...

LET'S WRITE... TODAY I AM GRATEFUL FOR...

Enjoy every moment.

WHAT ARE YOU CONFIDENT DOING?

Draw or write.

CAN YOU CARTWHEEL?

Cartwheeling is a rite-of-passage, like riding a bicycle or drawing. Being able to cartwheel can help YOU gain that all essential **CONFIDENCE** that can *spill over* into the rest of your life. It can give YOU self-assurance, pride, and belief in your own abilities to succeed.

It applies to everything that might seem hard or impossible. When YOU have a positive attitude, are determined to succeed, and *practice*, you will realize that YOU can do ANYTHING.

When it comes to **CONFIDENCE**, the more success you achieve, the more determined you become. The higher your confidence and the better you feel about yourself, the happier you will become. It's a powerful pattern.

CONFIDENCE in life is KEY.

CAN YOU DRAW CARTWHEELS?

Draw yourself or someone else doing a cartwheel.

CHECK OUT THE CARTWHIRLER™

This is the first and only TOY cartwheel mat that teaches kids ages **4-12+** how to cartwheel.
This mat has magical powers!
It teaches kids to believe in themselves, strive to reach a goal, fall and get back up, and learn to never give up.
It helps to build confidence, grow self-esteem, and encourages hours of independent play.

Find out more about this new product/toy/tool at www.CARTWHIRLER.com.

It's a carefully designed mat that teaches the proper hand and foot placement to CARTWHEEL.
It builds CONFIDENCE and smiles along the way.

Start here OFF the mat

↑ HAND   ↑ HAND   ↑ FOOT   ↑ FOOT

MY JOURNAL PAGES

MY JOURNAL PAGES

MY JOURNAL PAGES

MY JOURNAL PAGES

Letter-Writing Made Easy!

STEPS TO LETTER-WRITING

1. Tear or cut-out one of the template pages.
2. FOLD the envelope along the dotted lines.
3. Decide to WHOM you will write your letter.
4. Write on the envelope:
   From: _____ (your name and your camp address)
   To: _____(full mailing address of the person to whom you are writing your letter)
5. Add a postage stamp.
6. Write your letter on the opposite side.
7. Consider drawing or sketching a picture and adding it into your envelope using the tear or cut-out blank pages in this book. If you decide to do this, add a sticker at each side of the envelope to keep your picture from sliding out.
8. Put a sticker on the flap at the back to close your envelope. (You will need 3 stickers for each letter.)
9. Mail your envelope(s) or have someone deliver them.
10. Have fun letter-writing!

IDEAS:
- If you are going to a **sleep-away camp**, consider folding (and stamping) some template pages **in advance** ... **before** you leave for camp ... so these will be ready for you to use when you are there.
- Remember to bring stickers to close the DIY envelopes.
- Think about *SHARING* envelopes with your camp friends.

TO WHOM SHALL I WRITE MY LETTER?

Dear_____

- Mom
- Dad
- Brother
- Sister
- Friend
- Aunt/ Auntie
- Uncle
- Cousin
- Grandma/ Granny/ Nana/ Nan/ Bubie/ Oma/ Safta/ Teta/ Abuela/ Nonna/ MeMaw /GiGi/ YaYa/ MiMi/ Memere
- Grandpa/ Gramps/ Popa/ Pops/ Zeide/ Opa/ Saba/ Gedo/ Abuelo/ Nonno/ MePaw /Pop-Pop/ Gramps/ Pepere

- Other?

Date _____

Dear _____

BODY of letter

Hugs to you!
From _____

Okay ...
Let's all write!
Let's all draw!
Let's all sketch!
Let's all think!
Let's all be grateful!
Let's all have fun!

FOLD

From: _____

_____

_____

To:

_____

_____

_____

_____

FOLD

Stamp

CAMP FUN!

HI, FROM CAMP!

Date: _____

Hello _____ (Mom, Dad, Brother, Sister, Friend, Aunt, Uncle, Cousin, Grandma, Grandpa, Other)

I'm having a _____ (good, fantastic, amazing) time at camp!

The names of my camp counselors are _____

_____.

The names of the friends in my group or cabin are _____

_____.

The first thing we do is _____.

For lunch, I had _____ .

My best activity today was _____

_____.

Hugs   _____
             (your name)

FOLD

From: _____

_____

_____

To:

_____

_____

_____

_____

Stamp

FOLD

CAMP FUN!

I'M HAVING FUN AT CAMP! YES!

Date: _____

Hello _____

I'm having a _____ (*good, great, fantastic, amazing, incredible*) time at camp!

We are doing a lot of **FUN** activities! See the checks beside the things I have done so far!
- ____ Arts and Crafts
- ____ Baseball
- ____ Dance
- ____ Drama
- ____ Gymnastics
- ____ Hiking
- ____ Music and Singing
- ____ Performing
- ____ Playing games
- ____ Relay races
- ____ Obstacle courses
- ____ Soccer
- ____ Tie Dye
- ____ _____
- ____ _____

My best activity so far was _____ because _____.

Hugs

_____
(your name)

FOLD

From: _____

_____

_____

To:

_____

_____

_____

_____

Stamp

FOLD

CAMP FUN!

CAMP IS SOOOOOO MUCH FUN!

Date: _____

Hello _____

I am having a _____ (*good, great, fantastic, amazing*) time at camp!

The absolute most FUN thing I like to do is _____.

My counselor's name is _____.

My friend's name is _____.

On RAINY days, we _____.

The DANCE activity I like the most is _____.

My best MORNING activity is _____.

My best AFTERNOON activity is _____.

How are you? How are you doing at home? Hope you are good!

See you soon!

Hugs!

_____

FOLD

From: _____

_____

_____

To:

_____

_____

_____

_____

Stamp

FOLD

CAMP FUN!

I'M STAYING SAFE AT CAMP!

Date: _____

Hello _____

Things are going well for me at camp. I _____

_____.

My friends and I especially love to _____

_____.

Let me tell you a story of what happened: _____

_____

_____

_____.

My absolute best thing I like to *EAT* is _____.

The *SPORTS* activity I enjoy here is _____.

How are you doing? Hope you are all fine at home!

Hugs!

_____

From: _____

_____

_____

To:

_____

_____

_____

_____

Stamp

CAMP FUN!

HELLO, FROM CAMP!

Date: _____

Hello _____

I am having fun at camp! The game I recently enjoyed playing was _____.

Here's what happened: _____

_____.

My newest friend is _____.

We like to _____

_____.

Let me tell you something interesting that happened recently. _____

_____

_____

_____.

The *SPORTS* activity I enjoy playing here is _____.

Hope you are all fine at home!
Hugs!
_____

FOLD

From: _____

_____

_____

To:

Stamp

FOLD

CAMP FUN!

IT'S ME FROM CAMP!

_____

_____

_____

_____

_____

_____

_____

_____

_____

_____

_____

_____

_____

FOLD

From: _____

_____

_____

To:

_____

_____

_____

_____

FOLD

Stamp

CAMP FUN!

DRAW OR SKETCH
to make your letters come alive!

Following this page, you will find *blank* pages for you to use for drawing or sketching some pictures to include with your letters.

1. Along the folded line, tear or cut-out the blank page.
2. Fold it *twice* just like you did with the *Do-It-Yourself* (DIY) envelope.
3. Draw or sketch your picture. *Hope you have your colored pencils or markers. If not, sketching with just a pencil is fun too! Add shading with the side of the pencil.*
4. Insert your picture into the DIY envelope.
5. Use a sticker to close each side of the envelope so that your illustrated pages do not slip out.
6. Make sure you also put a sticker on the flap to close the envelope (so you will need 3 stickers in total for each letter).
7. Don't forget the stamp.

WHAT CAN I DRAW OR SKETCH TO ADD TO MY LETTERS?

Draw or sketch a picture of:

- you at camp
- you and your friends
- your newest friend
- your counselors
- you eating your most-loved food
- an animal or bird you see at camp
- an insect you see close up
- a tree
- you doing a camp activity
- you cartwheeling
- you skipping with a friend

- other?

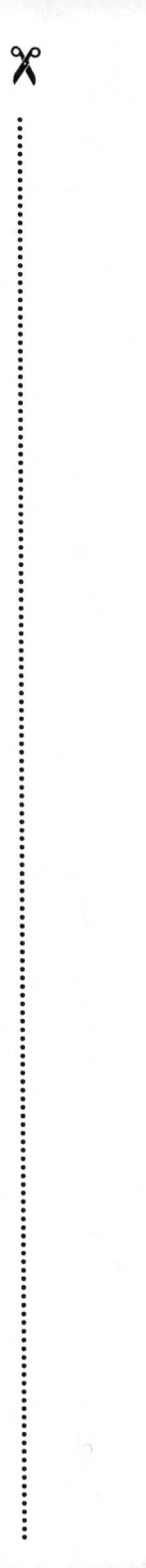

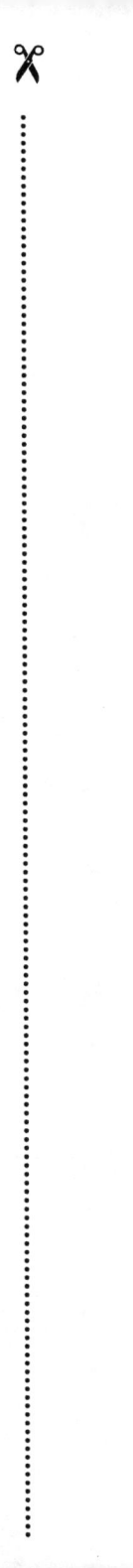

CAMP MEMORIES
Things to remember....

MY BIGGEST LEARNING:

MY PROUDEST MOMENT:

THE FUNNIEST THING THAT HAPPENED:

CAMP MEMORIES

Things to remember....

THE PERSON WHO HAD THE MOST IMPACT ON ME:

THE PERSON WHO TAUGHT ME THE MOST:

THE PERSON WHO I WANT TO CONTINUE TO BE FRIENDS WITH AFTER CAMP:

THE BEST DAY EVER:

AUTOGRAPHS

Ask your friends and counselors
to sign this page with their name.
Ask for their contact information if you don't have it.

AUTOGRAPHS

Continued...

AUTOGRAPHS

Continued...

AUTOGRAPHS

Continued...

WOW! YOU DID A LOT OF FUN THINGS AT CAMP!

Before you head home, remember to:

- Clean up your area.
- Pack up all your belongings.
- Collect things from your friends that you have lent them.
- Return anything that you have borrowed.
- Thank your counselors.
- Get the contact information for your new friends.
- Say good-bye to everyone.
- Make sure you have water and a snack for the ride home.
- Be grateful for the good times you have had.
- Have a big smile on your face when you meet your family.
- Look forward to the next time you come to camp.
- Look forward to next year!

Acknowledgments

Warm thanks to our mom, **Dr. Susan Schwartz** for helping us write and publish this book (www.creatingthedynamicclassroom.com). You are the most incredible role model. Thank you for teaching us to dream BIG, be lifelong learners, work hard, be resilient, and that any challenges we may face just can't stop our *ViBE*.

Love and thanks to our kids, **Samara, Sydnee, Jonah** & **Shayne**, for your interest and enthusiasm every step of the way. Love to our nieces, **Mia** & **Eliana**, too. We love you all more than words can say.

Thanks to Marnie's wonderful husband, **Sender Deutsch** (www.shapetoronto.com) for your enthusiasm, love, and support.

Acknowledgments to **Marc Henein, Alex, Alyssa,** & **Crosby** who brightened our lives at just the right moment.

Special thanks to **Alyssa Henein, Nicole** & **Kyla Lazarus**, and to **Lindsay Reeboh** for your help in field-testing this book and for your good ideas.

Thanks to **Ari Hochman** for your unending support with technology, ideas, and love.

Warm thanks and hugs to ALL of the **staff, dancers, and parents at *ViBE* Dance and Fitness Studio** (www.vibestudio.ca) over the past 20+ years.

Sending love and good vibes!
Marnie and Rena

About the Authors

Marnie & Rena Schwartz:
Twinsational Dancers, Performers, Certified Teachers, Accessibility Champion Award Winners, Dance Studio Owners/Artistic Directors of **ViBE Dance & Fitness Studio** in Thornhill, Ontario (www.vibestudio.ca), and Co-Creators/Inventors of the **CARTWHIRLER™** (www.cartwhirler.com).

This unique CAMP Activity WORKBOOK will be engaging and fun for campers to use all summer long. It is great for day camp and sleep-away camp.

Check out their other books (available on Amazon):

- EMPOWER YOUR ViBE, Igniting Your Passion, Purpose, and Brand to Unleash Your *Unstoppable* Best Self

- THE ViBE CONFIDENCE-BUILDING SERIES FOR KIDS, Ages 7 to 12
    - Book #1: You can DRAW CARTWHEELS, An Interactive Book about DRAWING and CONFIDENCE to Help YOU Draw Faces and People in Action

    - Book #2: I CAN Cartwheel, An Interactive Story about CARTWHEELING and CONFIDENCE Where YOU Become the ILLUSTRATOR

    - Book #4: FEEL THE ViBE From A to Z, An Interactive Workbook & FUN Card Game Focusing on POSITIVE AFFIRMATIONS & ALPHABETICAL ORDER

LET'S ViBE TOGETHER

We are passionate about making a difference and connecting with you, so please share your dance and cartwheeling stories and any photos, videos, or messages. Tag us on our social media platforms @vibedanceandfitness or @twwinzschwartz, or connect with us at info@vibestudio.ca or marnie@vibestudio.ca or rena@vibestudio.ca for any reason including to:

- Invite us as guests to be interviewed and/or to present or speak on your podcast or at an in-person or online event.
- Pump up any party or celebration by involving the participants in a dance and fitness class along with an inspirational talk and/or question/answer session.
- Book an engaging ViBE birthday party or celebration.
- Arrange for a fun dance and fitness class for your class or school. *Note ViBE's dance classes meet the expectations of the Ontario Dance Curriculum for multiple age and grade levels.
- Access consulting support about dance and fitness or cartwheeling.
- Implement Cartwheel Clinics at your dance or fitness facility.
- Receive support in using the CARTWHIRLER Cartwheel Mat.
- Inquire about becoming an Affiliate of our CARTWHIRLER products.
- Bulk purchase this book (or any of our publications) for your company, association, organization, school, or conference.

Check out our Linktree

To receive updates about our publications, and/or to check out our Useful Resources and Speaking Engagements along with other information about our business, product, and author brand, go to **https://linktr.ee/marnie_and_rena** or scan the QR CODE.

We Would Appreciate Your Review.

If you found this book or any of our publications and resources useful, we would greatly appreciate you writing a review and posting it on a platform of your choice (Amazon, Ingram Sparks, Goodreads, Google). Reviews make a big difference in helping to spread the word and assist readers in finding good books. Thank you for sharing your good vibes. It means more to us than you will ever know.

www.ingramcontent.com/pod-product-compliance
Lightning Source LLC
Chambersburg PA
CBHW081121080526
44587CB00021B/3701